Model Airplanes

By David and Ed Radlauer

AN ELK GROVE BOOK

 CHILDRENS PRESS, CHICAGO

Created by Radlauer Productions, Inc. for Childrens Press

Library of Congress Cataloging in Publication Data

Radlauer, David.
  Model airplanes.

  (Ready, get set, go)
  "An Elk Grove book."
  SUMMARY: Photographs and simple text introduce
the techniques of building and flying model airplanes.
  1. Airplanes—Models—Juvenile literature.
[1. Airplanes—Models] I. Radlauer, Edward, joint
author. II. Title.
TL770.R19   629.133′1′34   75-28032
ISBN 0-516-07465-2

1 2 3 4 5 6 7 8 9 10 11 12 13 14 15 R 82 81 80 79 78 77 76

Ready, Get Set, Go Books

Ready

Motorcycle Mania
Flying Mania
Skateboard Mania

Get Set

Fast, Faster, Fastest
Wild Wheels
Racing Numbers

GO

Soap Box Racing
Ready, Get Set, Whoa!
Model Airplanes

You can build and fly an airplane.

You'll be on the ground, but your model airplane will be up there flying.

Some people buy a model airplane that's ready to fly. Others say it's more fun to build one from plans. A balsa wood model is good, and it's easy to build.

Balsa wood is good because it's very light and easy to cut. Most other woods are too heavy to make model planes.
A model plane that's too heavy won't fly.

It's best to begin with a simple model airplane kit. But simple or not, a kit takes more work than money.

A kit has plans for building the model and most of the parts you need. The plans tell you what to do, and they have patterns to help you shape the balsa wood parts.

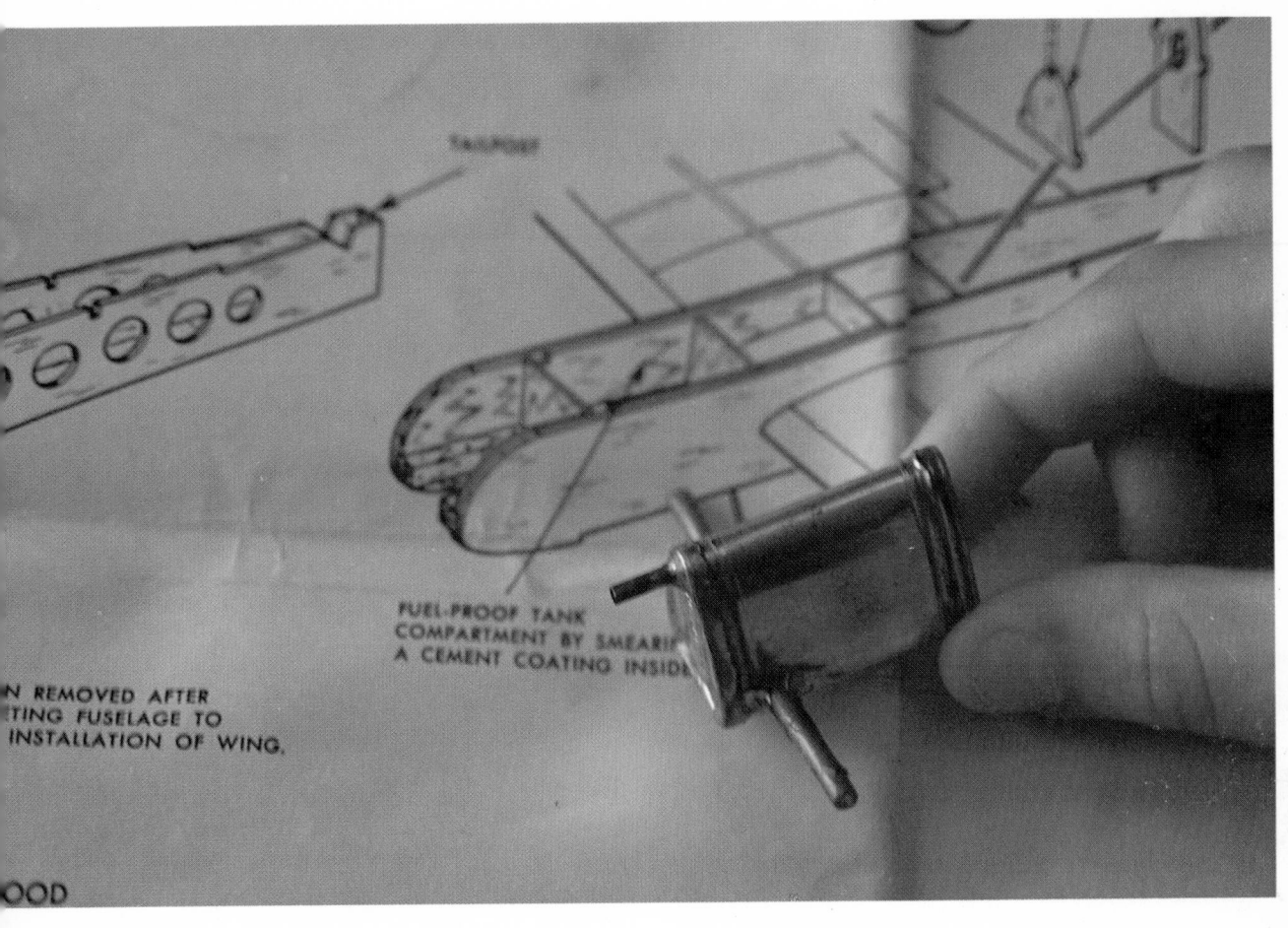

The pattern shows you the shape of
the parts. It also tells you how to put
the airplane together. And it shows where
to put the fuel tank and other parts.

Your model needs an engine. If your kit comes without an engine, you will have to buy one yourself.

Be careful to match the engine
to your model. If you don't match the
engine to the size of your airplane,
it may be too heavy. A heavy plane may
not get off the ground.

Ask a friend who flies model planes if you need a muffler. The muffler cuts down engine noise. Because of the noise, there are some places where you must have a muffler before you can fly a model plane.

The plans show you how to build
a wing and a body. The body is called the
fuselage. Both wings and the engine
connect to the fuselage.

Not all planes have fuselages. This plane is all wing with no fuselage. Why do you think the engine on this flying wing is set off to one side?

Your plane needs a strong engine mount. The mount has to be strong because a heavy engine can shake loose or vibrate off.

Here's what can happen when an engine
shakes loose and vibrates off the plane. This
engine took the mount with it. Does this look
like a good way to fly?

After your plane is built, it's ready to paint. The paint doesn't make your plane fly any better, but it does make it look like a real airplane.

Your first model is finished. The
paint is dry and it looks really great.
Now let's see. Will it really fly?

To find out, go to a grassy place where people fly model planes. Make sure there's nothing but grass for your airplane to run into.

Lay out the control lines and the control handle. The lines from the control handle connect to the bell crank. The bell crank moves the flaps on the wings and tail. By moving the wing and tail flaps you make the plane go up or down.

A good model flyer can show you how
to use the handle to control your plane.
To go up, pull back on the top of the
control handle. Pull back on the bottom
of the handle to go down.

Once your plane is flying, you'll have to learn the hard part—landing. The hard part is learning to make a soft landing.

You'll soon learn that landing takes more than just pulling back on the bottom of the control handle. Would you call this a soft or a hard landing?

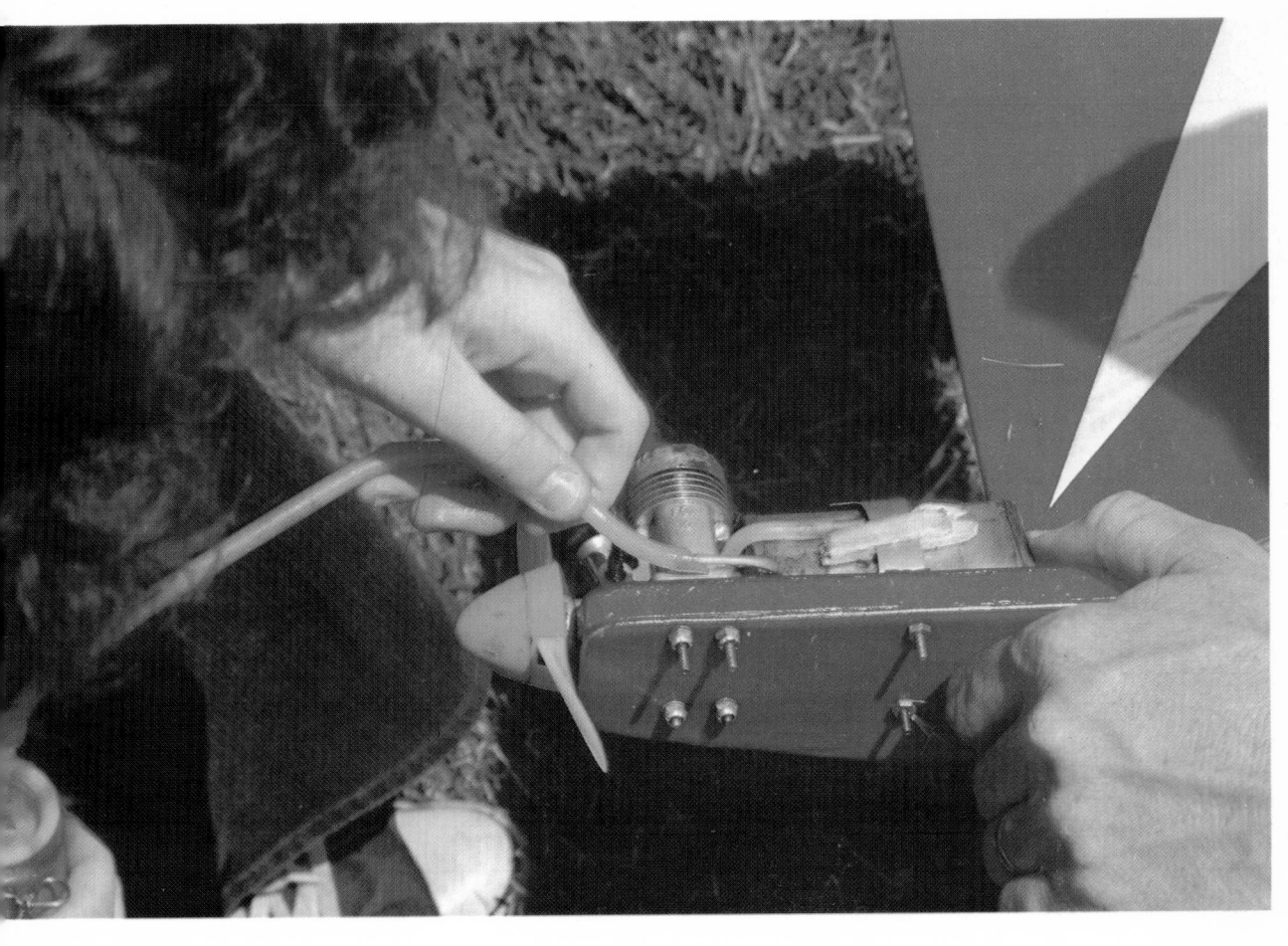

Before each flight, fill the tank with model airplane fuel. As the engine runs, it sucks fuel from the tank. When the fuel runs out, the engine stops and the flight is over. It's time to land.

A battery heats the glow plug for
engine starting. Spin the propeller
to start the engine. As soon as the engine
starts and the propeller is spinning,
take the battery wire off the glow plug.

Before takeoff, tune the engine to run at top speed. Tuning the engine for top speed gives the best flight.

During starting and tuning watch your fingers. A spinning propeller is good for flying, but not for fingers.

Have a friend hold the plane while you
run to the control handle. When you have
the control and you think you're ready,
tell your friend, "Let it go!" Then pull
back on the control handle for the takeoff.

You made a good takeoff and it flies!
You built an airplane that goes 60
miles per hour!